SOCIAL ANXIETY

AND SHYNESS

LEARN HOW TO BUILD SELF-ESTEEM, IMPROVE YOUR SOCIAL SKILLS AND OVERCOME FEAR, SHYNESS, AND SOCIAL ANXIETY

By Susan Brighton

TABLE OF CONTENTS

INTRODUCTION

Most of us often feel insecure, but some of us also feel relaxed. You may all have experienced social anxiety, fear, and insecurity through your kind of upbringing, past abuse, recent failure, or rejection encounters, isolation, social anxiety, negative attitudes about yourself, perfectionism, or having a critical parent or spouse.

Social anxiety disorder (verbal phobia) is an intense and recurrent fear of social environments. It is one of the most prominent anxiety disorders today. The disease of social anxiety is something more than "shyness". It can cause extreme anxiety and panic over basic daily tasks, such as shopping or talking on the phone.

Many people often worry about such social situations, but someone with a social anxiety disorder is going to worry about them constantly before, during, and after. They're afraid to do or say anything they think would be awkward or humiliating, like blushing, sweating, or being inept.

Social anxiety disorder is a complicated kind of phobia. This form of phobia affects a person's life in a destructive or impairing way. It can seriously affect a person's self-esteem and trust, interfere with relationships, and hinder work or school results.

The condition of social anxiety frequently begins during childhood or adolescence and appears to be more common in women. It's a known condition that can be handled successfully, so if you think you have it you should see your health provider.

The great news is, here is a great book that can help you overcome your insecurity, fear of facing people, low self-esteem, and social anxiety.

CHAPTER 1
WHAT IS SOCIAL ANXIETY?

Social anxiety (social phobia) is an overwhelming and long-term fear of social situations.

It is a common problem which usually begins in teenage years. It can be very distressing and significantly impact your life.

It gets better for some as they get older. But for many people it doesn't go away on its own without treatment. If you show any of the symptoms it is important to get help. There are treatments which can help you manage.

Symptoms of Social Anxiety

There is more to social anxiety than shyness. It's a fear that doesn't go away and affects daily activities, self-confidence, relationships, and work life or school life.

Lots of people occasionally worry about social situations, but before, during, and after them, someone with social anxiety feels overly concerned.

You may have social anxiety, if you show the following:

- Concern for daily events, such as meeting strangers, roughing, talking on the phone, shopping, or working.
- Worrying about or avoiding social activities, such as group conversations, company lunches, and parties
- Always worrying about what you think is embarrassing, such as blushing, sweating, or being incompetent
- Trouble doing things when others watch – you might feel like you're being watched and judged all the time
- Fear of being criticized, avoiding eye contact or lack self-esteem
- Frequently experiecing symptoms such as feeling sick, sweating, trembling, or heartbeat.
- Having panic attacks, where you have an overwhelming sense of anxiety and fear, usually for couple of minutes.

7

Lots of people with social anxiety also have other mental health problems, including depression, generalized anxiety disorder or panic disorder.

When to Get Help

In case you think you have social anxiety it's a good idea to see a GP, especially if it has a big impact on your life.

This is a common issue and there are treatments that can help.

Apparently, it can be so difficult to ask for help, but your physician will be aware that many people are struggling with social anxiety and will try to make you feel comfortable.

In knowing more about your anxiety in social situations, they will ask you about your feelings, behaviors, and symptoms.

If they think you might have social anxiety, they will refer you to a mental health specialist to have a full evaluation and talk about treatments.

You can also contact an NHS psychological therapies service (IAPT) directly without a referral from a health care provider.

You can try to get over social anxiety

Self-help can help reduce social anxiety and may be a useful first step before you try other treatments.

The following tips could be of great assistance:

- Try to know more about your anxiety – thinking or writing down what's going on in your mind and how you're acting in certain social situations can help you keep your diary
- Try some relaxation techniques, such as stress respiration exercises
- Divide the challenging situations into smaller parts and work with each part to feel more relaxed
- Try to focus on what people say, instead of simply assuming the worst

Social Anxiety Treatments

A number of treatments to address social anxiety are available.

The main options are:

- *Cognitive behavioral therapy (CBT)* with a therapist that helps you identify and change negative patterns of thinking and behaviors. This can be carried out in a group or with your parents or guardians, with just you and a therapist.
- *Guided self-help* involving working via a CBT-based workbook or online course with regular therapist support.
- *Antidepressant medicines*, typically referred to as the selective serotonin reuptake inhibitor (SSRI), such as escitalopram or sertralin. Usually these are not used to treat persons under the age of 15.

CBT is generally considered the best treatment but if it doesn't work or you don't want to try it, other treatments may help.

Some individuals need to try out a combination of treatments.

Social Anxiety in Children

Apparently, social anxiety can also affect children.

Signs of childhood social anxiety include:

- To cry or get upset more often than usual
- Getting very angry
- Don't interact with other children and adults
- Afraid of going to school or participating in classroom activities, school performances and social activities
- Don't request help at school
- Being very dependent on their parents or caregivers

If you're worried about your child, talk to your health care provider. They will ask you about the behavior of your child and will talk to them about how they feel.

Social anxiety treatments in children are similar to those for adolescents and adults although medicines are not normally used.

Therapy will be tailored to the age of your child and will often involve assistance from you.

Training and self-help materials may be given to you for use between sessions. It may occur in a small group, too.

CHAPTER 2
HOW TO OVERCOME
SOCIAL ANXIETY

We now live in an era of anxiety. It comes as no surprise that many people have experienced and still experience social anxiety with a mixture of numerous failures in the news while being bombarded by constant ads.

It is normal in ordinary, everyday circumstances and some might even say good to be nervous, after all it can help us perform better. Also, feelings of fear are intended to help us endure stressful circumstances that we may experience. Back in the days, this made us quicker to respond to the danger of being eaten alive; causing us to run, hide or throw a stone for those who are a little more courageous... (and then lay it down!) This reaction is known as the 'fight-or-flight' response that triggers the heart to speed up, hyperventilation (getting more oxygen) and increased muscle blood flow.

If we have to talk in front of a large group of people, we all get a bit nervous, right? Or is it the first time we have to meet someone? That is perfectly normal. There are numerous ordinary circumstances like this that cause people suffering from social anxiety to become cripplingly nervous and experience the fight-or - flight reaction that may be truly disabled in their daily lives. In a nutshell, social anxiety (social phobia) is the fear of social situations.

Coping with social anxiety can be stressful and progress doesn't happen overnight as with many things. You may feel like your mind is able to jump one million steps into the worst-case scenario instantaneously! Signs of social anxiety include:

- Find yourself concerned about responses from other people
- Experience extreme anxiety and nervousness when engaging in social situations
- Always felt uncomfortable for what you say and do in social situations

- Felt nervous
- Felt unnecessarily appraised
- Avoid all social conditions
- Experience physical effects on the body during social interactions such as sweating, heart rate changes, or fast breathing.
- Avoid eye contact

TIPS IN OVERCOMING SOCIAL ANXIETY

1. SHARE

Hiding or reducing anxiety does in fact create more anxiety. The most helpful move is to share your experiences with friends and family, or even speak to us or anyone else you trust about them online. Many people also feel embarrassed and can be extremely hesitant to share their anxiety. The media also lead people to believe that mental illness is a weakness which makes people less able to admit what they are going through to themselves and others. However, we all have mental health and it is estimated that as many as 1 out of 3 will experience a mental health condition at some stage and it's okay to talk about it.

2. *BREATHE*

Your body is strong. Then, it is so crucial to learn the warning signs of when your anxiety shows up to help you take action; for some, it could be your body feeling stressed and your mind feeling chaotic. It can improve your body, and especially your lungs. Exercises to relax will help you regulate your anxiety. Having a steady breath impacts your heart rate directly, and in turn, your emotions. Your heartbeat will slow down as your breath slows down and your mind and emotions will slow down so as your breathing and heart rate.

3. *QUIT NEGATIVE THOUGHTS*

As much as it feels you are being dominated by fear, fear is not reality and you control your own reality. Recalling that social anxiety feeds on thoughts that emphasize danger and fear is important. Symptoms like a rapid pulse and sweating come out of this kind of thought. Fortunately thinking is a habit, and can be modified, of course. The cure is not only a optimistic thought but a practical thought. Try to analyze your negative thoughts such as 'I'm going to say something dumb' which are mostly truth exaggerations. Then strive to generate thoughts critical of them and correct them.

4. ALWYAS SHIFT YOUR ATTENTION

Anxiety has a tendency to capture your attention and turn it inward on yourself, not just making you self-critical but also realizing how your pulse has risen rapidly without your permission, meanwhile, you then immediately feel warm, red in the face ... sweating ... it feels like a domino effect that can not be stopped. But instead, try to concentrate your attention on what you should do, so if you're talking to someone, try to pay close attention to what they're saying instead of thinking about what's right next.

5. FACE YOUR FEARS

In this particular moment, avoiding social interactions, yes would make you feel better. But note, this is only a short-term solution that prevents you from learning how to cope, and will make you more likely to avoid future social situations. As out of control as it might seem, you'll be able to work through the more difficult circumstances and teach you coping skills in the face of your fears in small measures. If you feel anxious to meet new people you may start by going to a party with a friend. You can now follow the next step of explaining yourself to a new person. Note, saying no each time you will get the same result. Saying "yes," however scary, means you take a chance and live your life.

6. *DO NOT TRY TO BE PERFECT*

We all live in a world that aspires to perfection; however, no-one is perfect. Also, do not forget that not everyone is going to like us and not everyone needs to. Press YOU do like everyone (slim chances)? It is also often forgotten that making mistakes is good, because it makes us human.

7. *ACCEPT REJECTION*

The game's purpose is to gain some form of rejection through a series of various challenges. The purpose of this rejection game is to allow you to see rejection differently and to face your fears while keeping some element of control over the situation.

Challenges for Beginners:

- Ask someone you normally don't talk to at school about the time
- Raise your hand to provide answer to question in class
- To praise others
- Initiate a chat with someone outside your friendship circle

Challenges for Intermediate:

- Demand a discount upon check-out
- Ask others to take a picture of yourself
- Ask your highest professor for an extension to your assignment, even though you don't need one
- Call an old friend and ask if you should make up
- Ask to go ahead of a queue
- Charity fundraising (* cough * we 're a charity * cough *) and telling people you know to help you

Challenges for Experts:

- Go to the restaurant and order a cooking tour
- Ask for a refill on a meal you have just eaten
- Dance open to the public.

CHAPTER 3
BUILDING SELF-CONFIDENCE AND OVERCOMING SHYNESS

Shyness is an apprehension and awkwardness that a few people feel while drawing nearer or when being drawn nearer by other individuals. These individuals want to outgo and to associate with others on a social and passionate level. In any case, they locate this inconceivable on the grounds that they can't deal with the anxiety that accompanies human connection.

It's imperative to bring up that shyness isn't equivalent to being contemplative. Loners really feel stimulated investing energy alone doing their very own thing. They aren't apprehensive about social gatherings, yet rather essentially want to be independent of anyone else. Social gatherings channel them inwardly, while lone exercises empower and flash their inventiveness.

Interestingly, bashful individuals urgently look for the acknowledgment and endorsement of others. This makes them incredibly reluctant and fearful of being judged, mocked, mortified, humiliated, and dismissed. They have a negative self-distraction and regularly assess themselves and their own capacity in constraining ways. Truth be told, with regards to social gatherings they expect that they will commit errors and bomb hopelessly to associate with others on an important level. Their unhelpful contemplations and convictions about their social connections make them feel very shaky. But then, one of their most charming qualities — that of being an astute audience — is an indispensable piece of any significant social relationship.

The Consequences of Shyness

Being overwhelmed with shyness is never useful for your social development and growth. In addition to the fact that it causes you to intentionally maintain a strategic distance from social gatherings, it can likewise prompt disengagement, pity, dejection, lament, and gloom. Indeed, every time you maintain a strategic distance from a social gathering, you are right then and there draining your supplies of fearlessness. Furthermore, the less self-assurance you have, the more uncertain you are to give your assessment, to make new companions, to exploit social chances to advance your vocation or accomplish your ideal goals.

We as a whole, have objectives and goals that we might want to accomplish. It's lamentable for modest people that by far most of these targets require the assistance of other individuals. This implies to carry their objectives to realization they should wander out into the world and make social associations. If really that they can't do this, at that point, they will wind up carrying on with a real existence brimming with second thoughts and unfulfilled guarantees.

These results can prompt a dangerous life. And also, it doesn't have to be like this. On the off chance that shyness is right now coordinating your choices and activities, at that point, it's not very late to roll out some significant improvements beginning today. The voyage, obviously, won't be simple, and it will require some investment and exertion. Be that as it may, with a craving to roll out these improvements stick and a promise to overhaul your social skills, you can unquestionably turn your life around.

Important Steps In Overcoming Shyness

Getting over shyness is not an easy task. This isn't a simple procedure. There are numerous anxieties and fears in the mix, and in that capacity, you might just need to work through every one of them exclusively. In any case, as with everything that is of worth, you will absolutely gain ground insofar as you're industrious and pursue the procedure well ordered.

Here is the four steps procedure you can use in overcoming shyness:

1. Gain Clarity

Your absolute and initial step is to understand what it is you might want to accomplish. Your ideal goals ought to at first be extremely basic and clear. For example, you may set an objective to pose an outsider an inquiry. After this underlying experience, you could set another objective to have a two-minute discussion with an outsider. At that point from that point, you would set extra objectives that will enable you to gain much more ground.

Ask yourself:

- *What is my main goal?*
- *What might I want to have the option to do socially?*
- *What is my underlying objective going to be?*
- *How can I get the ball rolling?*
- *What goals must I logically set to get to my ultimate goal?*

It doesn't lies what your objective is, the length of you are clear about it and it causes you become increasingly positive about social gatherings. Your true objective, obviously, maybe to interface and system with several individuals at a systems administration occasion at some point later on. In any case, you will positively need to gather speed logically after some time before this occasion, or else, you may wind up being hit with fear and anxiety on the day.

Having recognized your objectives, you should now recognize the snags that are right now keeping you away from making positive strides pushing ahead. Ask yourself:

What explicitly is keeping me away from accomplishing my main goal?

What is my opinion about this?

With regards to shyness your impediments are frequently psychological and internal. You might just have unhelpful reasoning styles that are ruling your idea examples, or you could have restricting convictions about a specific social gathering, or it could boil down to extremely limit desires for the social gathering you are in. It's significant that you are clear about every one of these deterrents before pushing ahead.

Ask yourself:

- *What exactly am I thinking about with regards to this social situation?*

- *What explicitly am I saying to myself about the social gathering or potentially about my capacity to deal with this gathering?*

- *How is talking and thinking with myself along these lines harming me?*

- *What about what I believe in?*

- *What do I believe about this social situation?*

- *What do I accept about myself in this situation?*

- *What do I expect will happen when I enter this social situation?*

Responding to these questions will furnish you with a deep comprehension of your mental propensities with regards to this specific social event. The more noteworthy clearness you have about these things, the more viably you will almost certainly work through these detours effectively.

2. Challenge Your Assumptions

It's currently time to take the appropriate responses you investigated in the past advance and start testing your suspicions. We are obviously expecting that the manner in which you're considering this specific social gathering isn't down to earth or supportive, and in that capacity, there must be a superior method to contemplate these potential situations. Investigate these conceivable outcomes by *asking yourself:*

- *Is this a practical way to see things?*
- *Am I possibly disregarding or ignoring the realities?*
- *By what other means can I view this social situation?*

It's truly conceivable that you are basically not seeing things obviously. You may, indeed, be seeing the gathering in a ridiculous and unhelpful manner. There could possibly be things that you're sitting above, and this is making you feel unconfident, fearful and restless.

If that you think that it's hard to see the gathering from an alternate perspective, at that point, it's significant you search out other individuals' conclusions, viewpoints, and perspectives. Locate a confided in a companion who makes you feel great and secure, and approach them for their sentiment and viewpoint about the social gathering you are battling with. Request that they help you see the gathering through their eyes. Rationally stroll in their shoes for a minute and experience what they are encountering as they clear their path through this social gathering.

The more supportive points of view you accumulate about this social gathering through your very own investigations and by asking other individuals, the to a lesser extent a hold your constraining convictions and unhelpful reasoning propensities will have over your choices and activities. In any case, regardless of whether after this, you are as yet feeling to some degree reluctant and hesitant, at that point, *ask yourself:*

- *What's the most terrible that could occur?*
- *In what capacity can I handle this worst scenario?*

- *What's my strategy?*
- *Who could possibly help me to get past this?*

The most terrible that could happen isn't as awful as you portray it. Truth be told, the worst-case situation will seldom happen. If it does happen, at this point you will get ready for whatever happens. This by itself can enable you to pick up the important certainty you have to step forward towards beating your sentiments of shyness.

3. Take Small Steps

You should now be prepared to make little steady strides day by day towards your ultimate objective. You should, obviously, start gradually and gather speed after some time. This is significant. Hopping into things too early can rapidly raise your anxiety levels, and accordingly, you will promptly withdraw into your usual range of familiarity. To stay away from this situation, make certain to set reasonable desires.

Regardless of whether you set aside the effort to completely get ready for this social gathering, it would even now be sensible to expect that you will feel somewhat on edge and that startling difficulties may emerge. This is alright. It's alright to feel restless. Anxiety will enable you to raise your degrees of readiness. Truth be told, all that you accomplish just because, or even things that you haven't accomplished for quite a while are frequently loaded with anxiety and somewhat strain. These enthusiastic encounters will in the end pass. It will take sometime and you should increase some involvement. The more experience you gain, the more prominent the certainty you will marshal pushing ahead.

As you make arrangements to everyday strides towards your end goal, set aside an effort to think about the following:

- *What particularly will I do socially today?*
- *By what means will I do this thing?*
- *Where exactly will I do it?*
- *Who will possibly be there?*
- *To what extent will I do it for?*

When drawing up your strategy, it's completely fundamental that you think about every one of these questions. These questions will enable you to be quite certain about the little advances required to arrive at your true objective. For example, you can decide to go to the general store and ask three outsiders questions about a thing in their shopping basket. You will do this in the shopping passageway, and you will collaborate with every individual for a sum of 30 to 60 seconds.

When you have accomplished your objective for that day, compensate yourself and plan to make another positive stride pushing ahead the extremely following day. Notwithstanding, make confident that tomorrow you do somewhat more. Perhaps tomorrow you will talk with five individuals and ask them a few questions about things inside their shopping basket. Possibly you could even set an objective to converse with them for as long as 90 seconds one after another.

As mentioned in the previous pages, sudden and unexpected things will occur. Individuals won't generally be receptive to your questions. A few people may, actually, be in a surge and would prefer not to hit up discussions with arbitrary outsiders. Other individuals may have an extremely terrible day, and therefore, they may be inconsiderate or disregard all of you together. Try not to accept this as an individual attack. These individuals are not out to get you. They are just having an awful day and being inconsiderate, and once in a while, pernicious is a useful method to discharge some strain. Simply overlook these individuals. Leave and discover another person you can interact with.

4. Learn From Your Experience

The last advance of this procedure is to gain from your experience. You may, in this manner, return home after your shopping endeavor at your nearby grocery store and plunk down with a pencil and cushion and work out your considerations, sentiments, and perceptions. Truth be told, here are a few questions you may get a kick out of the chance to pose to yourself about your experience:

- How did things go today?

- Did I achieve what I set out to do?

- What worked out well for me?

- Where did I encounter?

- What surprising difficulties did I face?

- How could I handle these difficulties?

- By what other method would I be able to have dealt with these difficulties?

- How may I have improved things if it happens again?

- What will I do in a different way tomorrow?

- What would I be able to improve tomorrow?

There are numerous questions you could possibly ask. Ideally, these questions can prompt you to get started.

However, in the end, the most significant thing is to take in the exercises from the experience you had today, and after that to present those exercises into your tomorrows. That is the main way you will learn and develop and gain ground to conquer shyness.

Preparing Yourself for Social Situation

There are many things you can do every day that will enable you to feel more positive, self-confident, and confident when it comes to placing yourself into social events.

Let's go through some of these things in a little detail:

- *Fortify/Strengthen Your Physiology*

Your body usage affects how you feel. How you feel affects your perceptions, and this, in turn, affects the choice you make and the actions that come with it.

At the point when in a modest perspective, you will in general be reluctant. You will take in a shallow way and your developments will be amazingly mindful. How are you regularly going to gain any ground socially if that you approach social gatherings along these lines?

Rather than being in a shy state, be certain. Truth be told counterfeit your certainty. Have you at any point known about the maxim: "counterfeit it till you make it"? All things considered, living along these lines can be fairly helpful. Consequently, as opposed to moving your body like a bashful individual would work on moving your body as if you were certain and secure in your own skin.

Ask yourself:

- How can a confident individual move his/her body?

- How can a confident individual stand?

- How can a confident individual sit?

- How can a confident individual act in social gatherings?

- How about facial expressions?

- What can they look like?

The responses to these questions will give you the rules you have to make the important acclimations to your physiology. It is insufficient to simply know these things, really set aside some effort to get ready and work on moving unhesitatingly from the start without anyone else, and later when in the organization of others. In case you need assistance, at that point essentially close your eyes and picture yourself in your creative mind as being confident about social gatherings. Regardless of how it turns out, don't stop there. Additionally, envision being brave, inquisitive, persistent and hopeful. These qualities will help change your physiology and help you to approach social gatherings with undeniably more certainty and confidence.

At first, these progressions will feel unnatural and constrained. In any case, after some time you will really increase genuine certainty, and that is the point at which you will never again feel as if you're moving or acting unnaturally. Your certainty will basically turn into a piece of who you are in social gatherings.

- ***Remain Calm Under Pressure***

At the point when in social gatherings, you will tend to feel somewhat on uncertain and anxious. It's normal becoming overpowered with anxiety. In any case, it shouldn't be like this as long as you prepare ahead of time.

Learning all you could about how to keep your feelings and emotions cool, collected, and calm during stressful situations. This basically comes down to building up the important enthusiastic adapting skills you will require when looked with analysis, dismissal and when you commit social stumbles or errors.

You should confront the way that you will be rejected and you will commit errors. It's significant not to harp on these things. These things are a piece of life and a piece of development and improvement. Gain from them and proceed onward. Your past is just there to enable you to settle on better choices later on, not to make you feel hopeless about yourself right now.

There are numerous things you can do to keep yourself engaged, focused, and aware of the present minute. One of these procedures is called dynamic muscle unwinding. It very well may be utilized now and again to help quiet your body and focus your psyche. It works by logically loosening up each muscle of your body beginning from your toes and completing at the tip of your head. It's something that is best practiced resting, anyway it should likewise be possible holding up. Simply close your eyes for a couple of minutes and see as a flood of quieting vitality ventures from the earth into your toes and up through your body.

During these minutes, you are attracting your consideration regarding the present. You are never again considering what others will think, say, or do. Rather, you are concentrating on being aware of existing apart from everything else. Also, this is the thing that will help quiet your feelings and enable you to assemble your considerations and travel through the social gathering with far less passionate change.

- *Avoid Perfection*

There is nothing of the sort as flawlessness. You will never be flawless. You can just do your absolute best, and your absolute best will bring about altogether different results relying upon the day and the social gathering you end up in.

Try not to be challenging for yourself when you commit errors. Mix-ups are a typical and characteristic piece of life. Truth be told, the main way you'll learn is the point at which you commit errors. It's each of the learning procedure that requires some investment, persistence, commitment, and exertion. You will, in the long run, arrive, and you won't be immaculate. That is superbly typical. No one is flawless, regardless of how things show up superficially.

- *Do Not Compare Yourself to Others*

Contrasting yourself with other individuals when you're deficient in certainty will just discourage you and make you feel totally hopeless. Rather, contrast yourself with as well as can be expected be. Furthermore, even as well as can be expected be will be distinctive on various occasions. Everything you can do is attempt your best and after that, gain from this experience to improve whenever around.

- *Try not to Label Yourself as Being Shy*

Marking yourself as being shy will frequently bring about acting modest. Rather name yourself as certain, enthusiastic and intentional in your activities. Consistently you venture out into this world you are on a mission. There is genuine reason and explanation for every one of your activities. You have objectives to accomplish and activities, and cooperating with others on a social level is only an aspect of your responsibilities.

Keep in mind that the marks you give yourself are simply convictions. Some of the time these convictions are of your own creation, while different occasions they depend on other individuals' desires for you. For example, other individuals may have disclosed to you more than once that you're modest. At first, you probably won't have named yourself thusly. Notwithstanding, after some time as an ever-increasing number of individuals marked you as being shy, you have started to accept this, and your underlying thoughtful nature has transformed into a social phobia that is meddling with your vocation.

If that you have a lot of restricting convictions that are making you see yourself as a bashful individual, at that point work through these convictions without anyone else's input or chat with somebody about them. Ask a nearby and believed companion to scrutinize this conviction to help toss question in your brain about the legitimacy of accepting and thinking along these lines.

- *Educate Yourself*

Invest some energy and time teaching yourself about how to improve your social skills, your ability to handle conflict, and your social manner. Discover what you should do to turn out to be progressively confident and assertive. Additionally, become familiar with human instinct and non-verbal communication (body language)

These skills will help improve your comprehension of social circumstances. Moreover, they can help furnish you with the assertiveness that you deserve to work through social problems effectively.

CHAPTER 4
WHAT IS IRRATIONAL
FEAR?

Nearly everybody has this awful feeling, for example, your every year dental checkup. For many people, these feelings of trepidation are minor. Yet, when fears become so serious that they cause colossal anxiety and meddle with your ordinary life, they're called phobias.

Phobia is known to be an extreme fear of something that, in actuality, has little or no real damage. Basic phobias and fears involve heights, driving, flying insects, needle, snakes, and confined space. You can create phobias of essentially anything. While most phobias create in youth, they can likewise create in later life.

In case you have a phobia, you most likely understand that your fear is nonsensical, yet despite everything you can't control your sentiments. Simply pondering the feared article or gathering may make you restless. When you're really faced with that thing that gives you fear, this fear is programmed and overpowering. It experience is so nerve-wracking that you may put forth an admirable attempt to keep away from it—burdening yourself or notwithstanding changing your way of life. On the off chance that you have claustrophobia, for instance, you may turn down a rewarding employment proposition on the off chance that you need to ride the lift to get to the workplace. If that you have a fear of statures, you may travel an additional 20 miles so as to keep away from a tall scaffold.

Understanding your phobia is the initial step to beating it. Know that phobias are normal. (Having a phobia doesn't mean you're insane!) It likewise realizes that phobias are exceptionally treatable. Regardless of how crazy it feels at the present time, you can conquer your anxiety and fear and begin carrying on with the existence you need.

Natural Fear Versus Irrational Fears

It is typical and even good to experience fear in hazardous situations. Fear fills a defensive need, initiating the programmed "battle or flight" reaction. With our bodies and brains caution and good to go, we can react rapidly and confident ourselves. Yet, with phobias, the risk is non-existent or significantly not well presented. E.g., it is just normal to fear a growling Doberman, yet it is unreasonable to be alarmed of a benevolent poodle on a chain, as you may be if that you have a pooch phobia. A lot of childhood fear is normal, and these fears are developed at a specific ages.

Natural Fear for Children

For instance, lots of kids are scared of the dark and may require a nightlight before they can sleep. This doesn't imply they have a phobia. However, they will grow out of this as they develop mentally and age-wise.

Let take a look at some common and normal childhood fears:

-   **0-2 years** – Strangers, large objects, separation from parents, loud noises.

-   **3-6 years** – Imaginary things like strange noises, ghosts, darkness, sleeping alone.

-   **7-16 years** – Realistic fears such as illness, death, school performance, natural disasters, etc.

If your kid's fear isn't meddling with their everyday life or causing them a lot of misery, at that point, there's little reason for undue concern. But, if the fear is meddling with your children's social life, sleep, or their [performance in school, then you might need to see a professional kid specialist.

Common Types Fears and Phobias

There are four different types of phobias and fears:

1. Animal phobias, for example, the fear of dogs, snakes, rodents, and spiders.

2. Natural condition phobias, for example, a fear of storms, heights, dark, and water.

3. Situational phobias, that is, fear activated by a particular situation, including the fear of closed

spaces (claustrophobia), driving, flying, bridges, and tunnels.

4. Blood transfusion-Injection-Injury phobia, the fear of injury, needles, illness, and other medical engagements.

A few phobias, be that as it may, don't can be categorized as one of the four regular classes. These incorporate fears of stifling, fear of getting an illness, for example, malignant growth, and fear of jokesters. Other basic phobias that don't fit flawlessly into any of the four classifications include:

Social phobia, likewise called social anxiety issue, is fear of social gatherings where you might be humiliated or judged. If that you have social phobia, at that point you might be exorbitantly unconfident and scared of embarrassing yourself before other people. Anxiety over some things such as, what others will think of you and how you will look may lead you to maintaining a clear distance from certain social gatherings you'd generally appreciate.

Fear of open talking—an amazingly regular phobia—is a sort of social phobia. Different apprehensions related with social phobia incorporate fear of drinking, eating in broad daylight, interacting during a social gathering, writing test in school, communication with someone you don't know or being approached in office.

Agoraphobia was generally thought to include a fear of open places and open spaces; however, it is currently accepted to create as an intricacy of fits of anxiety.

In case you're apprehensive about having another panic attack, you become on edge about being in gatherings where getaway would be troublesome or humiliating. For instance, you're probably going to keep away from swarmed places, for example, shopping centers and cinemas. You may likewise maintain a strategic distance from trains, vehicles, planes, and every other type of movement. In extreme cases, you may just have a sense of security at home.

Signs and Symptoms of Phobias

The manifestations of a phobia can go from mellow sentiments of misgiving and anxiety to an out and out panic attack. Ordinarily, the closer you are to the thing you're anxious about, the more prominent your fear will be. Your fear will likewise be higher if escaping is troublesome.

Physical side effects of a phobia include:

• Difficulty relaxing

• Racing or beating heart

• Chest agony or snugness

• Trembling or shaking

• Feeling bleary-eyed or discombobulated

• A beating stomach

• Hot or cold flashes; shivering sensations

• Sweating

Emotional side effects of a phobia include:

• Feeling overwhelming panic or anxiety

• Feeling the deep need to getaway

• Feeling detached from yourself

• Fear of going crazy or losing control

• Feeling like you're going to die

• Knowing that you're going overboard, yet feeling feeble to control fear

Signs and Symptoms of Blood-Injury Phobia

The signs of blood-injection phobia are somewhat not quite the same as every other phobia. At the point when defied with seeing blood or a needle, you experience fear, yet in addition, sicken.

Like different phobias, you at first feel on edge as your heart accelerates. In any case, in contrast to different phobias, this quickening is trailed by a speedy drop in pulse, which prompts sickness, discombobulating, and blacking out. Albeit a fear of blacking out is normal in every single explicit phobia, blood-infusion damage phobia is the main phobia where swooning can really happen.

Overcoming Fear/Phobia

Self-help techniques and treatment can both be compelling at treating a phobia. What's best for you relies upon components, for example, the seriousness of your phobia, your entrance to proficient treatment, and be confident of help you need.

When in doubt, self-help is constantly worth an attempt. The more you can accomplish for yourself, the more in charge you'll feel—which goes far with regards to phobias and fears. In any case, if your phobia is extreme to the point that it triggers fits of anxiety or wild anxiety, you might need to look for extra help.

Treatment for phobias has an incredible reputation. In addition to the fact that it works incredibly well, yet you will, in general, get results all-around rapidly—some of the time in as a little as one to four sessions. In any case, support doesn't need to come in the pretense of an expert specialist. Simply having somebody to hold your hand or remain close by as you face your feelings of fear can be incredibly useful.

1. Face Your Fear, Slowly

It's just normal to need to maintain a strategic distance from the thing or gathering you fear. With regards to eliminating your phobias, confronting your feelings of fear is the key. While evasion may make you feel better temporarily, it keeps you from discovering that your phobia may not be as startling or overpowering as you might suspect. You never find the opportunity to figure out how to adapt to your feelings of fear and experience authority over the gathering. Accordingly, the phobia turns out to be progressively scarier and all the more overwhelming in your psyche.

The best method to defeat a phobia is by bit by bit and over and again presenting yourself to what you fear in a sheltered and controlled way. During this presentation procedure, you'll figure out how to ride out the anxiety and fear until it unavoidably passes. Through rehashed encounters confronting your fear, you'll start to understand that the most exceedingly terrible won't occur; you're not going to kick the bucket or "lose it." With every introduction, you'll feel increasingly certain and in charge. The phobia starts to lose its capacity.

It's essential in any case a gathering that you can deal with, and stir your way up from that point, constructing your certainty and adapting skills as you climb the fear ladder.

- *Create a list:* Make a rundown of the terrifying gatherings identified with your phobia. In case you're apprehensive about flying, your rundown (notwithstanding the self-evident, for example, taking a flight or overcoming departure) may incorporate booking your ticket, gathering your bag, heading to the airplane terminal, watching planes take off and land, experiencing security, loading onto the plane, and tuning in to the airline steward present the wellbeing guidelines.

- *Develop your fear ladder:* Organize the things on your rundown from the least startling to the most unnerving. The initial step should make you marginally on edge, however not all that scared that you're too threatened to even think about trying it. When making the stepping stool, it very well may be useful to consider your ultimate objective (for instance, to have the option to be close hounds without freezing) and after that separate the means expected to arrive at that objective.

- *Make your way up the fear ladder:* Begin with the initial step and don't proceed onward until you begin to feel increasingly good doing it. If that conceivable, remain in the gathering long enough for your anxiety to diminish. The more you open yourself to the thing you're apprehensive about, the more you'll become accustomed to it and the less restless you'll feel when you face it whenever. When you've done a stage on a few separate events without inclination a lot of anxiety, you move onward to the following stage. If that a stage is excessively hard, separate it into littler advances or go slower.

- *Practice:* The more regularly you practice, the speedier your advancement will be. Be that as it may, don't surge. Go at a pace that you can oversee without inclination overpowered. What's more, recollect: you will feel awkward and restless as you face your apprehensions, yet the emotions are just brief. On the off chance that you stick with it, the anxiety will blur.

2. Learn To Calm Down

When you're apprehensive or on edge, you experience an assortment of awkward physical indications, for example, a hustling heart and a stifling inclination. These physical sensations can be alarming themselves—and a huge piece of what makes your phobia so troubling. In any case, by figuring out how to quiet yourself down rapidly, you can turn out to be progressively confident about your capacity to endure awkward sensations and face your feelings of fear.

Play out a straightforward profound breathing activity. When you're restless, you will, in general, take speedy, shallow breaths (known as hyperventilating), which really adds to the physical sentiments of anxiety. By breathing profoundly from the midriff, you can switch these physical sensations and feel less tense, less shy of breath, and less restless. Practice when you're feeling quiet until you're comfortable and alright with the activity.

• Sit or stand easily with your back straight.

• Take a good amount of air in through your nose.

• Hold your breath for some minutes.

• Exhale through your mouth to a tally of eight, pushing out as much air as you can while getting your muscular strength.

• Inhale once more, rehashing the cycle until you feel loose and focused.

• Practice this profound breathing method for five minutes twice daily. When you're OK with the method, you can utilize it when you're confronting your phobia or in another distressing gathering.

3. Challenge Negative Feelings About Your Phobia

When you have a phobia, you will, in general, overestimate how terrible it will be in case you're presented to the gathering you fear and think little of your capacity to adapt. The on-edge considerations that trigger and fuel phobias are typically negative and unreasonable. By recording the negative musings you have when gone up against by your phobia, you can start to challenge these unhelpful perspectives. Ordinarily, these contemplations fall into the accompanying classifications:

- ***Fortune telling:*** For instance, "This scaffold is going to fall;" "I'll make a trick of myself without a doubt;" "I will lose it when the lift entryways close."

- ***Overgeneralization:*** "I blacked out once while getting a shot. I'll always be unable to get a shot again without going out;" "That pit bull jumped at me. All canines are risky."

- ***Catastrophizing*** "The commander said we're experiencing disturbance. The plane is going to crash!" "The individual by me hacked. Possibly it's swine influenza. I will become ill!"

When you've known your negative feelings or thoughts, assess them. You can use the following listed examples to get started.

It's likewise useful to create some positive statements that you can tell yourself when being faced by phobia. For instance:

• "I've felt this type of way before, and nothing awful occurred. It might be awful, yet it won't hurt me."

• "If the something terrible occurs and I have a panic attack while I'm driving, I'll basically pull over and hang tight for it to pass."

• "I've flown countless times, and the airplane has never crashed. However, flying is so safe."

CHAPTER 5
WHAT IS LOW SELF-ESTEEM?

Low self-esteem is described by an absence of certainty and feeling gravely about oneself. Individuals with low self-esteem frequently feel unlovable, ungainly, or bumbling. As indicated by specialists Morris Rosenberg and Timothy J. Owens, who composed Low Self-Esteem People: A Collective Portrait, individuals with low self-esteem will, in general, be extremely touchy. They have a delicate feeling of self that can undoubtedly be injured by others.

Moreover, individuals with low self-esteem are "hyper-vigilant and hyper-alert to indications of inadequacy, rebuff, and rejection, according to Owens and Rosenberg. Most times, people lacking confidence and self-esteem see disapproval and rejection even when there is none. "The risk consistently prowls that they will do something embarrassing, expose themselves to ridicule, make a mistake, behave abhorrently or immorally. Life as a whole gives an everyday threat to self-esteem."

While everybody's confidence is defenseless against other individuals, who may transparently scrutinize them, disparage them, or bring up their blemishes, I would contend that a significantly more prominent danger to every individual's confidence prowls inside. Rosenberg and Owens clarify:

"As eyewitnesses of our own conduct, contemplations, and emotions, we register these marvels in cognizance as well as condemn them. Along these lines, we might be our most extreme commentator, chiding ourselves barbarously when we end up making a blunder in judgment, overlooking what we ought to recall, conveying everything that needs to be conveyed ponderously, breaking our most holy vows to ourselves, losing our poise, acting immaturely—to put it plainly, acting in manners that we lament and may lament."

This cruel internal faultfinder, which Dr. Robert Firestone alludes to as the Critical Inner Voice, adds to an apparent negative self. Having a negative impression of oneself can have genuine results. For instance, on the off chance that somebody accepts that other individuals don't care for them, they are meant to maintain a certain distance from relating with others and are speedier to respond protectively, critically, or even lash out. Rosenberg and Owen contend that "nature and degree to which we associate with others is firmly affected by these apparent selves, paying little heed to their exactness. To be confident, our apparent selves speak to one of the most significant establishments on which our relational conduct rests." Furthermore, when we see ourselves adversely, regardless of whether we name ourselves unbalanced, unlovable, repulsive, modest, etc. It is becoming increasingly hard to accept that others could see us in a positive light.

However, according to Owens and Rosenberg, "to have low self-esteem is to live a life of misery and hopelessness."

Overcoming Low Self-Esteem

Fortunately, it is completely conceivable to defeat low self-esteem! There are two key ways to combatting this negative mental self-image, namely:

- Quit listening to your inner critic

- Practicing self-compassion

1. Quit Listening to Your Inner Critic

The critical inner voice is that inner observer that destructively judges our actions and thoughts. This terrible internal critic ceaselessly bothers us with a blast of negative thoughts and actions about ourselves and the individuals around us. It annihilates our confidence or self-esteem on a reliable basis with thoughts like the following listed:

- *"You're dumb and stupid."*

- *"You're fat."*

- *"No one enjoys you."*

- *"You ought to be peaceful. Each time you talk, you simply make a fool of yourself."*

- *"Why can't you behave like other people?"*

- *"You're useless."*

So as to defeat low self-esteem, it is important that you challenge these negative feelings or thoughts and confront your inward pundit. On Psych-Alive, we have a whole segment of articles, a few Webinars and an e-Course committed to this subject. The initial step is to perceive when you begin thinking these sorts of negative contemplations about yourself. You can decide not to tune in to your inward pundit's character deaths or flawed guidance. It very well may be useful to envision how you would feel on the off chance that another person was directing these sentiments toward you; you'd most likely feel irate and guide them to quiet down or clarify that they are incorrect about you. Adopt this strategy in reacting to your inward pundit.

One approach to do this is to record all your inward pundit's reactions on one side of a bit of paper. At that point record a progressively sensible and merciful examination of yourself on the opposite side. For instance, in case you compose a self-analysis like "You're inept," you could then state, "I may battle now and again, yet I am shrewd and equipped from multiple points of view."

Testing your inward pundit helps stop the disgrace winding that feeds into low self-esteem. When you perceive the basic, inward voice as a wellspring of your negative self-attacks, you can start to challenge this internal pundit and see yourself for who you truly are.

2. Start Practicing Self-Compassion/Self-Empathy

From numerous points of view, the remedy for self-analysis and self-criticisms is self-empathy. Self-empathy is simply the extreme routine with regards to treating like a companion! It is a magnificent method to assemble more trust in yourself. Research has demonstrated that self-empathy is shockingly better for your psychological wellness than confidence.

Dr. Kristen Neff, who looks into self-sympathy, clarifies that self-empathy did not depend on self-assessment or judgment; rather, it depends on a relentless demeanor of graciousness and acknowledgment toward yourself. While this may sound basic, treating yourself with sympathy and thoughtfulness might challenge from the outset. Be that as it may, you will grow increasingly self-empathy as you practice after some time.

Here are the three stages for practicing compassion/empathy:

- Acknowledge and know your suffering

- Be caring and kind in response to suffering

- Always have it in mind that imperfection is something we all share, and it is part of human experience.

Developing Self-Confidence

Various studies on self-esteem show that both high and low esteem can bring about social and emotional problems for people. While abnormal states, confidence can be connected to narcissism (read increasingly here). Low degrees of confidence can be connected to social anxiety, absence of certainty, and discouragement. The most beneficial sort of confidence is moderate confidence that depends more on esteeming one's inborn worth as an individual and less about contrasting oneself with others. In this sense, if you will likely grow fearlessness progressively, it is smarter to concentrate on having large amounts of self-esteem as opposed to elevated amounts of confidence.

I've expounded in the previous chapter about building your self-esteem and growing more confidence. Aside from practicing self-compassion and challenging your internal critics alone, there are few other techniques/ways to feel better about yourself.

- *Quit Comparing Yourself to Other People*

Hoping to support your certainty by estimating yourself against others is a major mix-up. Dr. Kristen Neff clarifies, "Our aggressive culture discloses to us we should be uncommon or more normal to like ourselves, yet we can't all be better than expected simultaneously… There is consistently somebody more extravagant, increasingly alluring, or fruitful than we are." When we assess ourselves dependent on outside accomplishments, other individuals' observations and rivalries, "our feeling of self-esteem ricochet around like a Ping-Pong ball, rising and falling in lock-venture with our most recent achievement or disappointment." Social media just intensifies this issue, as individuals post their truly amazing minutes and glossy accomplishments, which we contrast with our discolored, imperfect regular daily existences.

So as to build a healthy self-esteem, we have to quit comparing ourselves with others. Rather than stressing over how you match up to the individuals around you, consider the kind of individual you need to be. Set objectives and take activities that are predictable with your own qualities.

- *Satisfy Your Own Moral Code*

Self-esteem and self-confidence are based on a sense of respect. On the off chance that you live a life that is in accordance with your very own standards and principles, whatever they might be, you are bound to regard yourself, feel increasingly confident, and even improve throughout everyday life. For instance, a study carried out at the University of

Michigan found that students "who put together their confidence such as, adhering to their moral standards or being virtuous, were found to get higher marks and less likely to develop a sleeping disorder or use drugs or alcohol.

To like yourself, it is essential to have trustworthiness and confidence that your activities coordinate your words. For instance, if eating well and putting your best self forward are significant qualities to you, you will feel much improved on the off chance that you keep up a solid way of life. At the point when your activities don't coordinate your words, you are unmistakably progressively helpless against self-attacks. The internal commentator wants to bring up these inadequacies. It is significant to consider your center standards and act in accordance with those convictions when you are attempting to support your certainty.

- *Do Something Meaningful*

As individuals, we will in general like ourselves when we accomplish something significant, partaking in exercises that are bigger than ourselves as well as helping other people. This is a lovely approach to building certainty and creating more beneficial degrees of confidence.

Researches show that volunteering positively affects how individuals feel about themselves. Analyst Jennifer Crocker recommends that you discover "an objective that is greater than oneself." When seeking after significant exercises, it is imperative to consider what feels the most critical to you. For certain individuals, this may mean volunteering at a destitute sanctuary, coaching kids, participating in nearby governmental issues, planting with companions, and so forth. Pursue the breadcrumbs of where you discover importance, and you may locate your confidence en route.

Increasing Self-Esteem Through Your Actions And Accomplishments

There's an inconsistency at the core of self-esteem. And on the other hand, everybody has intrinsic self-respect that doesn't rely upon their achievements or actions. Self-esteem originates from the inside. It's not something other individuals give on you, or a prize you win after you've done what's needed things to demonstrate to the world that you're commendable. Then again, self-esteem is somewhat influenced by what you do. It goes about as a measure for whether you're living such that is imperative to you and can't resist the urge to diminish if your life isn't in a spot you need it to be. It's only an aspect of human instinct that we care about these sorts of things.

Gaining self-esteem through your activities can be a tricky act. You can groom your self-esteem through what you do, however, there are traps you have to stay away from. You would prefer not to come to feel your self-esteem relies upon your achievements. I'll discuss that as we dig deeper into this book.

There are ways you can change your attitudes to impact your self-confidence:

- **Live Life on Self-Esteem Affirming Practices**

This is essentially what this chapter is all about. One thing your self-esteem does is determining whether you're carrying on with your life based on some key practices and alter itself as need be. This isn't a thorough rundown, however, when you reliably do things like the following listed below, your self-esteem will rise:

- Live life based on your own qualities or values
- Live in such a way that is self-constructive, for instance doing regular exercise.
- Think for yourself and pick your very own way through life
- Do work/make things that are significant and meaningful to you
- Take full responsibility for yourself and what bearing your life goes in
- Stand up for your right and treat yourself with respect.

When you shun these practices, you'll know it within you, and your self-esteem will reduce:

- Break or sell out your most profound qualities, for instance, valuing self-sufficiency.

- Live foolishly, for instance, abusing drugs
- Blindly following other individuals' idea and thoughts about how you should live
- Don't do work that feels significant to you
- Feeling people are responsible for your joy and happiness
- Let others mistreat you

By and large, you could contend standards like these are designed into individuals. I think everybody shifts in which ones they accentuate, however. For instance, one individual may feel a solid destroy to have a significant activity and lose confidence on the off chance that they're simply planning something for compensation the bills. Another person might be glad to take any old activity and put more significance on having an independent perspective. Living by these gauges takes steady work, and it's anything but difficult to accidentally be driven adrift, so not superbly satisfying them doesn't mean you're a finished disappointment. Give a valiant effort, and act naturally tolerating of the occasions you don't get them right.

*-   **Improve On the Areas You're Struggling With***

You can build your self-esteem by attempting to improve in any territories where you have shortcomings that trouble you. This is especially valid since individuals' self-idea is progressively influenced when they realize they're missing something significant, instead of when they increase a 'pleasant to have.' These shortcomings could be social issues like constant shy, poor conversational capacity, absence of empathy, dejection, etc. They could likewise be issues in different circles like your funds or profession bearing. Whatever your issues are, you should rest easy thinking about yourself once you get them leveled out. By and by, this is evidently a stage that will require significant investment, as you can't roll out clearing improvements to your life in a couple of days. Regardless of the fact that on the off chance that you were already directionless and debilitated, even simply having an essential 'activity plan' for how you're going to begin chipping away at your issues may improve your self-idea a piece.

- *Work To Create Positive Characteristics*

It's normal we feel a sense of self-respect or worth in the event that we have a few things going for us. Set aside some effort to build up your current positive characteristics, or work to achieve new ones. This could include attempting to develop certain parts of your character, or rehearsing to gain proficiency with another ability.

- *Challenge Yourself And Achieve Goals You Set For Yourself*

You can't resist the urge to feel increasingly certain in the event that you've had a few triumphs. Each individual will set various objectives relying upon what's critical to them. Testing ourselves additionally expands our sentiments of self-adequacy, that is the feeling that we're commonly adaptable and equipped and can deal with what life tosses at us.

- *Build An Environment That Supports Your Self-Esteem*

Everything being equal, who's likelier to have great self-esteem? Somebody who works a corrupting activity, and whose 'companions' and accomplice always put them down, or somebody who has steady, reassuring individuals throughout their life? Once more, on one level, your self-esteem shouldn't rely upon what other individual's state about you. We ought to have the option to ignore the mistaken, pernicious things they state. On another level, we're all human, and in case we're always undermined and offended, it can't resist the urge to influence us.

- *Keeping Away From The Pitfalls*

Like I said there are sorts of counter-productive reasoning you can fall into when you depend on outside achievements to build your self-esteem:

• You can begin to feel that your self-esteem relies upon accomplishing certain things. In the event that you can clutch a specific state (e.g., having a high-glory occupation), or keep consistently achieving specific objectives (e.g., having new individuals like you), then you like yourself. Generally, your self-esteem self-destructs.

• You can consider self-to be as something you contend over. In case you can beat other individuals in a specific zone, you 'win' it. In the event that they beat you, you lose it.

• Your accomplishments just give a brief lift to your confidence. After that, you feel uncertain again and need another fix.

• You can feel like you need to accomplish certain things so as to 'demonstrate' you're not a failure anymore.

• You can unwittingly develop an admired persona and dream life to pursue. You believe you're useless until you get that, and that in the event that you accomplish it you'll live cheerfully ever after.

Individuals who pursue other sources (external) of self-esteem most times rack up many achievements. Nonetheless, they're always unable to truly make the most of their successes.

Here are thoughts on avoiding these issues:

• You need a strong establishment of self-acknowledgment. In case you don't acknowledge yourself at a center level, at that point all that you do will be an endeavor to conceal or overcompensate for what you feel is your genuine defective self. This isn't to imply that you should put every one of your objectives on hold until you become 100% self-tolerating. Attempt to develop it at a similar you move in the direction of them.

• It knows about the false, unsafe messages I referenced before. Numerous individuals pursue outer wellsprings of self-esteem since they accept messages revealing to them they have to pursue these things.

• Try to know about for what reason you're making progress toward something. Might you be able to live without it, however it would even now be decent to have?

- *Dispute Any Self-Esteem Hurting Thinking You Have*

At a point, people have poor self-esteem they tend to have a misguided thoughts that continue it. For instance, somebody's colleague may not react to a content welcoming them to hang out, and they'll rapidly close, "This is on the grounds that they despise me. I'm a washout. I'll never have companions." You can avert a portion of that harm by figuring out how to perceive and debate these ridiculously up. This proposal is certifiably not a total technique for improving self-esteem all alone, yet it can help clean up your reasoning when joined with different methodologies.

- *Use Short-Term Self-Esteem Supports Sparingly*

As far as I can tell a portion of the proposals, you'll go over for raising your self-esteem extremely just give you a fleeting lift to your state of mind. Here and there we need to brighten ourselves up, however, so I don't see anything amiss with utilizing them for the intermittent lift me up. Be that as it may, while they help in a shallow manner, you can't simply up the dose to improve your actual self-esteem, close to gulping more Aspirin will recuperate a sprained lower leg. The procedures will either be an insufficient exercise in futility or become unfortunate propensities. The ones I can consider are:

- Taking time to help yourself to remember your positive qualities and achievements
- Positive certifications
- Taking on increasingly cheerful, certain non-verbal communication (standing upright, grinning)
- Dressing up and making yourself look decent
- Doing something to treat yourself

Fine in little doses, yet unhealthy whenever taken excessively far:

- Comparing yourself to others who are more regrettable off than you and acknowledging you don't have it so terrible
- Seeking consolation or approval from others

CHAPTER 6
ENHANCING YOUR SELF-ESTEEM

Self-confidence is used to allude to a couple of related ideas. At times, some people use it as an option to 'self-esteem,' that is, somebody's general assessment of their value. At different occasions when they talk about their self-confidence, they mean how confident, skilled, and valiant, they feel specifically social circumstances. These circumstances might be very broad, for instance, interacting with people you don't know very well or increasingly explicit, e.g., public talking.

In case you have strong self-esteem, that can stream down into your situational social confidence, and it never damages to take a shot at it. The two don't generally go together, however. There are individuals who are effective and sure at parts of socializing, however, who don't generally have a favorable opinion of themselves where it counts. There are additionally individuals who like themselves all in all, yet at the same time feel on edge and out of their profundity at whatever point they, state, need to go around and acquaint themselves with everyone at a major gathering. At any rate, it doesn't feel great to do not have this sort of social confidence, so I'll give my considerations on the best way to build it.

Regardless of whether you're attempting to develop the situational or self-esteem kind of confidence, you should have a couple of things you ahead of time, for example, confidence is highly significant in our everyday life, yet it is not everything.

- There are two kinds of situational confidence

I began this chapter by discussing how the term *self-confidence* can be analyzed further. Presently I will do something very similar to its situational sub-type. I've discovered when individuals feel situational confidence, they're feeling one, or both, of two potential outcomes.

- Logical knowledge, that is, ability to handle hand self-confidence
- Psyched up feeling

Logical Assessment of Your Capabilities

This is the way individuals feel when they're genuinely positive about their capacity to succeed. They 'know' they can perform in specific circumstances a similar way they realize the sky is blue. They may have a well-tried range of abilities or some other solid bit of leeway. Their dry, reasonable sureness likewise originates from having the option to think back on a string of past victories. This is a sort of confidence that must be earned.

Individuals who feel positive about along these lines have a practical feeling of what they're able to do and accept their devices are adequate to finish the current task. They don't really believe they're the best on the planet, similarly tantamount to they should be. Somebody who's just been playing tennis for a long time would at present feel tranquility sure they could beat somebody who's never held a racket. In the event that you have this sort of confidence, it likewise doesn't mean you never feel anxious or uncertain of yourself going into a circumstance. Anyway, underneath those regular feelings is a feeling of, "I'll be fine. I've done this kind of thing a million times. It, for the most part, works out. What's more, when it doesn't, I can manage it."

The Psyched up Feelings

As opposed to the past variety, this sort of confidence is very feeling based. Individuals encountering it fondle charged. They deliberately see how curiously sure they are. It's a decent sort of confidence to have. Somebody who feels along these lines going into a gathering is going be quieter, talk to more individuals, and seem to be more confident than somebody who's uncertain and down on themselves.

When somebody is sure, they'll do well they feel that quiet, consistent confidence. On the off chance that you know indeed you'll succeed, there's no compelling reason to get that passionate about it. Psych up confidence is bound to appear fully expecting occasions where the individual isn't so certain about their odds. An untested apprentice could encounter it, yet so could a veteran going into a surprising predicament. It resembles their psyche is attempting to amp them up so they'll have the option to confront the difficulties ahead.

The enormous issue with this assortment of confidence is that it's momentary and temperamental. In the event that it generally showed up when required, that would be incredible, however, it more often than not doesn't go down that way. There's no predictable strategy to bring it out on order, however, individuals once in a while have accomplishment with the accompanying techniques:

- Trying to psych themselves up physically, by tuning in to driving music, bouncing around, shouting rallying calls, beating their chest, and so forth.
- Listening to an energetic, inspirational discourse, or guiding one to themselves.
- Joking around with individuals to attempt to get themselves into a free, fun-loving state of mind.
- Trying to take a gander at the circumstance in an unexpected way, so it will appear to be simpler or lower stakes (e.g., considering it a potential learning knowledge, not decisive).
- Trying to discover a snippet of data that will make them bound to succeed, and along these lines feel all the more certain about themselves (e.g., a discussion subject that they're told will go over well with the group they'll be meeting).
- Getting other individuals to siphon up and energize them.

The issue is regardless of whether these strategies work they will, in general show extremely solid unavoidable losses. What fires you up the first run through never appears to function too again. On the off chance that it circumstance makes you unconfident, it makes you unconfident, and there's no idiot-proof momentary technique to get around that.

Here's a way a few people unexpectedly get diverted: typically feel unconfident and sketchy in a circumstance and don't perform well in it, however from time to time, for whatever strange reason, people get a burst of psych up confidence and show improvement over they regularly would. They justifiably start to consider that to be a passionate state as the way to their prosperity and begin pursuing it. They likewise begin to feel there's no reason for attempting except if they sense they will be psyched up. Like I stated, there's no real way to invoke this inclination voluntarily, so they wind up discarding their time and vitality.

Gradually Increase Genuine Ability And Comfort In The Areas You Feel Unconfident About

In the long run, the best approach to boost one confidence about a particular situation is to put in enough energy and time to be more comfortable and proficient in them. I discover different methodologies are simply celebrated approaches to attempt to call that passing psyched up inclination. Going this course means tolerating there will be a clumsy learning stage, where you won't feel especially sure, which you have to put yourself through at any rate. Exploit any psych up confidence as it springs up, yet don't feel subject to it. And what you actually need is to concentrate on having the option to delicately make yourself practice and work for the future regardless of whether you're not flooding with strength.

With regards to building specific social skills, you need a thought of what you have to do, and afterward, continue placing yourself in circumstances where you can rehearse them. And when you start getting the hang of things, you'll additionally begin to develop your own victories, which you can draw on for much more confidence. Expanding your solace levels is comparative. To manage the circumstances that truly make your apprehensive, you have to drive yourself to confront them, at a pace you can deal with. This book goes into the way, way more detail:

Self-Esteem and Social Situation

Particularly when you're beginning, your social skills and confidence can go here and there erratically. It tends to be truly befuddling and debilitating. I've heard individuals make statements like:

• "Why does my confidence and charm change such a great amount of every day? One day I'll be in an extremely confident, active mind-set, and have no issues conversing with anybody. Whenever I see similar individuals, I'll feel bashful and unreliable, and not have the option to string two sentences together."

• "What gives? Throughout the previous two weeks, I felt sure and agreeable around, dislike my standard timid self, yet now I'm all of a sudden shaky once more."

To be clearer on this, your self-confidence can absolutely swing here and there. And also, your social skills themselves don't change a ton medium-term, however, they're influenced by your confidence. A ton of shy individuals have preferable social skills and characters over they give themselves acknowledgment for. It's simply that more often than not they're excessively restrained or self-questioning to demonstrate their actual abilities. When they're feeling sure, those obstructions drop away.

There are heaps of reasons your confidence can teeter-totter, which this book will go into. Simultaneously, you frequently can't be absolutely certain why your confidence is going up or down in a specific minute. All the more significantly, you just have such a great amount of capacity to control how confident you feel. You will have great and terrible days. Once in awhile, you'll plunk down with your colleagues for lunch, and for no discernible reason, you'll be in a truly beguiling, well-disposed state of mind. At different occasions, despite the fact that you've utilized each persuasive stunt you know, despite everything you'll feel blundering and pulled back.

It's simply part of the way toward dealing with your social issues that your confidence can swing starting with one day then onto the next. You can burn through a ton of time attempting to discover a non-existent approach to feel 'on' continually. The main thing that truly works over the long haul is to reliably rehearse your relational and mental skills. In the end, you'll arrive at a point where your social confidence is all the more relentless. You'll show signs of improvement at disregarding difficulties. Regardless you'll have off days, yet they won't influence your presentation to such an extent.

I'll cover the reasons your confidence can bounce around as far as outside and inner elements. Obviously, there's some cover between the two, yet

I discovered this was a decent method to sort out every one of the focuses.

EXTERNAL FACTORS

- *The general arbitrariness of the social world*

This is a general factor. The social world's an erratic spot. It gives you a blend of empowering and disheartening circumstances. Regardless of whether you have astounding relational abilities, you can't absolutely control how other individuals act or treat you.

Your confidence can be tossed around by arbitrary occasions. You may go to a gathering and karma into five discussions in succession with individuals who truly appear to like you, and that will be sufficient to make you feel large and in charge for the following two days. On day three, you could appear at work and discover your associate is in a surly, standoff-ish state of mind, and think about it literally and begin to question yourself once more. Now and again it's one extra-demoralizing occasion that interferes with you. Once in a while, it's a progression of somewhat disillusioning experiences that include.

Once in awhile, you'll know precisely what association expanded or diminished your confidence. At different occasions, something will trigger a move, yet you won't know how it influenced you. For instance, somebody battles with self-esteem, and unknowingly gets down on themselves at whatever point they state 'yes' to things they would prefer not to do. In any case, intentionally just felt like they merrily consented to enable somebody to out, and after that bafflingly fell into a funk in the hours that pursued.

- *Having the chance to practice or not*

We will in general feel progressively sure and calm in circumstances when we're in them all the time and have had sufficient energy to get settled. You might feel progressively sure in light of the fact that you've been socializing reliably and have gathered up some speed. Outside conditions like occasions, sicknesses, or different responsibilities, can fend off you from everybody for some time. When you return, you learn about a touch of shape and apprehensive. In case you're not mindful you were sneaking out of shape, it might appear as though your confidence dropped all of a sudden.

- ***Getting the hang of one expertise/acknowledging there are different ones to learn***

For instance, from the onset, somebody battles to begin discussions with outsiders and make a couple of minutes of casual conversation. They invest the energy and show signs of improvement at it. When they understand things are fitting properly, they get a surge of confidence and utilize their new capacity each possibility they get. After a short time, they discover there are more preservation challenges past the casual chitchat arrange, and their confidence endures a shot as they battle with them. Mentally they knew there was in every case more to adapt, however, a little piece of them trusted, "When I become accustomed to visiting individuals I don't have the foggiest idea about the entirety of my social issues will be unraveled," and is let down to find that is not the situation.

- *Other life stressors or victories*

Your trust in any one zone is mostly influenced by the general measure of bliss or worry in your framework. Nothing might turn out badly on the social front, however then you do more awful than you expected to on a test, or get into a battle with your folks, or have your skin break out, and the pressure, anxiety, and self-question from those issues can eat into your confidence around individuals. Or on the other hand, the inverse could occur: You were feeling uncertain around your colleagues, however then discovered you found low maintenance line of work you truly needed. That rush may transmute into inclination loose in social circumstances.

- *How healthy or weak you're feeling*

Our state of mind and confidence is additionally impacted by how well our bodies are getting along when all is said in done. You may discover you feel a touch all the more certain about yourself around individuals when you're eating and resting soundly, getting some activity, aren't debilitating, and have relatively little on your plate. In the event that you take on a lot of work, and your rest, eating, and exercise propensities languish over it, you may begin feeling less certain around everybody.

- *Biological/Natural factors that can cause emotional episodes/mood swing*

Different conditions can cause emotional episodes when all is said in done, which may appear as your social confidence rising or falling. It's past the extent of the book to broadly expound on every one of them, however, I mean things like:

• If you're a young person, your fluctuating hormones

• If you're a lady, where you are in your menstrual cycle

• Having Bipolar Disorder

• Having Attention Deficit/Hyperactivity Disorder

• Being on the mental imbalance range

In case you're a young person or female, I'm making an effort not to say each and every, single thing you feel can be discounted to hormones or the way that you're PMS'ing. It's more that alongside the various elements, they may once in a while assume a job.

INTERNAL OR MENTAL FACTOR

A topic going through a great deal of these is that apprentices aren't as great at taking care of the inescapable good and bad times of socializing. Each and every achievement or disappointment can move how they feel about themselves.

-   You simply have a blend of social strengths and weaknesses

This one needn't bother with much clarification. Your blend of strong and not really strong skills will cause you to have a blend of results, that can make your confidence spike or plunge. For instance, you might be great at tuning in and getting some information about other individuals, however, get reluctant on the off chance that you need to discuss yourself. In the event that you talk to somebody who needs to do the majority of the talking, you'll have a smooth discussion and left away feeling sure. And in any case, you meet somebody who asks you a great deal of inquiries, you may quiet down, and feel like a botch after.

- *The tendency to see your present status as evidence of how the future will turn out*

This doesn't cause moves in your confidence level itself. What it can do is cause the swings you to have for different reasons to feel progressively extreme, depleting, and debilitating. Tenderfoots at a wide range of skills can fall into this psychological snare. I think individuals are likewise bound to surrender to it on the off chance that they're actually sincerely put resources into improving at something.

How it functions is that if things are going admirably - on the off chance that you have a couple of good discussions, or feel great at a gathering - you'll will in general think, "Yes! I've gotten the hang out this. It will be going great starting now and into the foreseeable future!" If you have an awful extend, your reasoning will flip to the similarly false untimely finish of, "Agh, it's sad! I'll never show

signs of improvement. I will resemble this eternity."
You can bob forward and backward between these
two attitudes, in light of what the social world tosses
at you.

- *Belief in an instant cure*

This likewise supports the power of any enthusiastic
high points and low points. Individuals who are first
attempting to get over their timidity or improve their
social skills regularly have the ridiculous desire for
a handy solution. The initial couple of times things
go well for them they get excessively energized and
think every one of their issues are settled. At that
point when something definitely turns out badly,
they crash down to earth. Once more, a few people
can invest a great deal of energy ping ponging
between sentiments of "I'm relieved! For genuine
this time!" and "Ugh, no I'm definitely not. Is it
consistently going to occur for me?"

- *Your shy counter-productive reasoning patterns*
reasserting themselves

A focal component of the condition is that shy,
unreliable individuals think in all sorts of self-

undermining ways. They're superfluously hard on themselves. They consider to be cooperation as being more hazardous than they seem to be. They reach off base inferences about what's to come. They accept a lot of accountability for occasions outside of their control. They consider others to be as being mean and judgmental. I could continue endlessly, yet these books really expound:

It's a long haul undertaking to distinguish and begin wearing down the maladaptive perspectives that feed your timidity and low self-esteem. In the event that you get a flood of confidence for one reason on another, those positive sentiments may incidentally push your self-attacking reasoning aside, however, it will return. Something won't go splendidly for you, and you'll translate it in a lot of cynical, reckless ways and slide once more into inclination unconfident. You may have been thinking in an uncertain style for ten years or more, you can't clear that away just by having a bunch of smooth discussions.

Indeed, even once you find out about your psychological mutilations and begin questioning them, you can at present waver from one side of the confidence scale to the next. That is on the grounds that by testing your musings you can beat some of them back, and perhaps briefly feel increasingly certain thus, however different contortions won't go down so effectively and will rally to sink your state of mind. Once more, you can't change your idea designs in half a month.

- *You're surfing a sequence of brief or short-lived psych ups*

As this book clarifies, there are two different ways somebody can feel certain:

1. True, earned trust in a territory, which feels like a consistent, calm, self-evident understanding of one's abilities.

2. A striking and bold, psyched up sensation, where you feel perceptibly more esteemed than expected. This sensation generally comes up when you're more uncertain of yourself in that setting.

Particularly when we're recently chipping away at our social skills, we can get ourselves into this psyched up state unintentionally. We may peruse an inspirational statement, or be journaling about our issues, and have an apparently significant revelation about what's been keeping us down, and afterward feel amped up, and like we can assume control over the world. It's helpful to fondle charged, yet the catch is this sort of confidence is brief and difficult to call up on order. Individuals can stall out in a cycle where they get psyched up for some reason, feel useful for a couple of days, at that point have it wear off and feel unconfident once more.

- *The urge of achieving something hard for the first time*

The first moment when you accomplish something, you were attempting to accomplish makes you feel emotionally high. That urge can change into a dash of confidence. For instance, you may feel astounding the first occasion when you ever converse with a companion on the telephone, if that was something that frightened you. As you can figure at this point, high wears off, and the sentiment of confidence and invulnerability with it.

- *Fear of success*

At times we realize we need to succeed in some parts of life, however when we're on the verge of getting through to that next level we get scared a bit and begin to question ourselves and agonizing over what could turn out badly. In the event that you've had a couple of good weeks socially, you may feel sure for some time, yet then work yourself out of it by intuition things like, "Who am I joking? I'm not intended to have great social skills. I'm the unusual, ungainly kid. This can't last."

- *You start pressurizing yourself as your confidence level goes higher*

You begin a couple of discussions with your colleague, not expecting anything of it in any case. Your visits go well, you begin resting easy thinking about yourself, and you keep on having great connections with them. At that point, you arrive at a point where you begin thinking, "We've been getting along well the previous couple of weeks. I can't mess this up. I can't return to my old conduct." That weight itself may make you lose your confidence, or it might lead you to act bashful and cumbersome, and that breaks your streak.

Obviously, there are bunches of reasons your confidence can rise and fall. Some of the time there will be an obvious issue you can recognize and fix, however, generally, you should attempt to acknowledge your confidence will vacillate, that it just accompanies being a novice and that you can't do a ton to transform it for the time being. Watch out for the long haul arrangement, which is to continue rehearsing, regardless of whether you aren't generally in the best headspace, to manufacture a genuine establishment of expertise and versatile reasoning.

CONCLUSION

The bottom line when attempting to break away from a rut of social anxiety is to note that it all takes time. Whatever changes you make in your life, you aren't going overnight from socially insecure to social butterfly.

Be pleased with every little progress you make; every journey starts with small steps and it's crucial that you start and don't think too much about your goal right now. Focus on the road and take your acts there.

Milton Keynes UK
Ingram Content Group UK Ltd.
UKHW051814060823
426331UK00020B/488